Feminist 𝕾𝖆𝖈𝖗𝖊𝖉 𝕾𝖔𝖓𝖌𝖘 for 𝕮𝖍𝖗𝖎𝖘𝖙𝖒𝖆𝖘

Carols for the
Twenty-first Century
Celebrate the Mystery of
the Intimate Presence of God

Edited by
Genia Pauli Haddon, D.Min., Ph.D.

—Feminist-Christian Resources Series—

Plus ✠ Publications

1994
Published by Plus Publications
Box 265, Suite 97
Scotland, Connecticut 06264 U.S.A.

Copyright © 1994 by Genia Pauli Haddon

Second Edition

"All Who Tell the Gospel Story" © 1980 Stephen C. Rose, used with permission.
"Lullaby for the Expected Child" © 1989 Irene Levine, used with permission.
"Child of the Living God" © 1992 Lorraine M. Nelson, used with permission.
"In Mary's Heart" words and chords © 1994 Genia Pauli Haddon; tune © 1994 Roberta Bitgood.

All rights reserved. Duplication of any portion of this publication without written permission from the publisher is a violation of Federal Copyright Laws.

> To make copies without permission is a form of theft.
> Please respect the years of work the author has put into this material.

Printed and bound in the United States of America.
10　9　8　7　6　5　4　3　2　1

Cataloging-in-Publication Data
Haddon, Genia Pauli, ed.
　　　Feminist Sacred Music for Christmas: Carols for the twenty-first century celebrate the mystery of the intimate presence of God
　　　　　1. Christmas music　2. Women's Studies

783.6 [Dewey System]

ISBN 1-881311-08-2

Christians of many varieties love these carols!

"What a way to celebrate the birth of the Holy Child—with a call to justice for all and an invitation to receive in new ways Emmanuel, God-with-Us."
—Paulette Harwood
M.Div. Seminarian, YALE DIVINITY SCHOOL

"For those of us who love Jesus, it is refreshing to find an expression of the mystery of the incarnation in such all-inclusive language."
—Mark Kelso (Hansaraj), KRIPALU YOGA disciple
Songwriter and recording artist
For God Alone; Cathedral; A Human Heart and others

"The image of Jesus is enhanced by the variety of metaphors. Each song is unique and gives a special touch to the sacredness of the season."
—Richard K. Walker
Ordained Deacon, ROMAN CATHOLIC

"Through WomanChurch, I outgrew the language of the old carols. But at Christmas I still want to sing! Now I can."
—Maria Santos
WOMANCHURCH-East

"If Christmas is your New Age holiday of choice, this collection of songs will delight you. These new carols are not just fun—they also help us integrate old and new wisdom... In fact, Plus Publication's entire *Feminist-Christian Resources Series* cannot be praised enough."
—Loretta Hoback
NEW AGE REVIEWER
Haight Ashbury Free Press; New Age Retailer

Dedication

*In Memory of all the
magical Christmases of our childhood,
with love to my brothers and sister:*

Sunny - Carl
Dicky - Richard
Kitty - Marie

Contents

	PAGE
Theological and Practical Guidelines	9
Advent Songs	15
Christmas Songs	23
Evening Program Outline	49
Acknowledgements	51
About the Author/Editor	52

Alphabetical Listing of Songs

	NUMBER
All Who Tell the Gospel Story Stephen C. Rose, contemporary. Tune: "Angels from the Realms of Glory"	26
Angels from the Realms of Glory James Montgomery, early 19th century; modified by Genia Pauli Haddon. Tune: REGENT SQUARE	9
Angels We Have Heard on High Traditional French carol; modified by Genia Pauli Haddon. Tune: GLORIA	11
Away in a Manger Anonymous; modified by Genia Pauli Haddon. Tune: Traditional	20
Bring a Torch, Jeannette, Isabella! Traditional carol, late 19th century; modified by Genia Pauli Haddon. Tune: Traditional	18
Child of the Living God Lorraine M. Nelson, words and music, contemporary.	27
Christians, Awaken! James Byrom, mid-18th century; modified by Genia Pauli Haddon. Tune: YORKSHIRE	25
Come, Thou Long-Expected Jesus Charles Wesley, 18th century; modified by Genia Pauli Haddon. Tune: STUTTGART	4
Creator of the Stars of Night Latin, anonymous, 9th century; re-written by Genia Pauli Haddon. Tune: "Just As I Am"	12
Good Christian Friends, Rejoice Traditional German carol, 14th century; modified by Genia Pauli Haddon. Tune: IN DULCI JUBILO	24
Hark! The Herald Angels Sing Charles Wesley, 18th century; modified by Genia Pauli Haddon. Tune: Traditiional	10

In Mary's Heart   14
Genia Pauli Haddon, contemporary. Tune: by Roberta Bitgood

In the Bleak Mid-Winter   16
Christina G. Rossetti, 19th century; modified by Genia Pauli Haddon. Tune: CRANHAM

It Came Upon a Midnight Clear   8
Edmund H. Sears, 19th century; modified by Genia Pauli Haddon. Tune: Traditional

Joy, Peace, and Love! The Gifts of Christ!   28
Genia Pauli Haddon, contemporary. Tune: "Joy to the World"

Joy to the World   6
Isaac Watts, late 17th century; modified by Genia Pauli Haddon. Tune: Traditional

Let All Mortal Flesh Keep Silence   22
Liturgy of St.James, 19th century; rewritten by Genia Pauli Haddon. Tune: PICARDY

Lift Up Your Heads   3
George Weissel, 17th century; modified by Genia Pauli Haddon. Tune: TRURO

Lo, How a Rose Ever-Blooming   13
German, anonymous, 15th century; re-written by Genia Pauli Haddon. Tune: ES IST EIN ROS

Lullaby for the Expected Child   5
Irene Levine, words and music, contemporary.

O Come All Ye Faithful   23
John F. Wade, mid-18th century; modified by Genia Pauli Haddon. Tune: Traditional

O Come, O Come Emmanuel   1
Latin, 9th century; minor modification by Genia Pauli Haddon. Tune: Traditional

O Little Town of Bethlehem   17
Phillips Brooks, late 19th century; modified by Genia Pauli Haddon. Tune: Traditional

Silent Night   21
Joseph Mohr, early 19th century; minor modification by Genia Pauli Haddon. Tune: Traditional

Wake, Awake!   2
Philipp Nicolai, late 16th century; modified by Genia Pauli Haddon. Tune: WACHET AUF

What Child Is This?   19
William C. Dix, late 19th century; modified by Genia Pauli Haddon. Tune: GREENSLEEVES

What Star Is This?   15
Charles Coffin, early 18th century; modified by Genia Pauli Haddon. Tune: PUER NOBIS NASCITOR

While Shepherds Watched Their Flocks   7
Nahum Tate, late 17th century; re-written by Genia Pauli Haddon. Tune: Traditional

If desired, divide singers into A and B groups, and follow the marginal cues for alternating voices.

Theological and Practical Guidelines

Do you remember how old you were when you first sang "Silent Night", "Joy to the World!" and "O Come, All Ye Faithful"? Such carols are simply in the air at Christmas time, to be taken in whole at an early age, without mature understanding, with little concern for the meaning of the words. These old carols are charged with all the emotional nuances of all your Christmases past. Because they were internalized pre-cognitively, the actual meaning of those words continues to escape conscious awareness—until we sing a version with a few changes! Then, perhaps for the first time ever, our minds awaken also to the full meanings of the familiar words.

The words of hymns and carols always communicate particular theologies—interpretations of the events they commemorate and the mysteries they attempt to communicate. Many traditional carols express a theology that elevates manly values while incompletely honoring the dignity of womanly insights. It is especially appropriate to explore the alternative perspective during Advent and Christmas, when we celebrate the intimate presence (rather than the superior distance) of the Divine. The revised Christmas songs in this book express the mystery of *God-with-us*, in terms consistent with that divine action.

Those who penned the original words held theological convictions which, while valid on their own terms, do not reflect equally valid theological insights developed in the years (or even centuries) since their times. Let's continue sometimes to sing and enjoy their classic words, even as we also discover the value of alternative nuances in these re-tellings of the Christmas event.

The intention in these versions is to honor and celebrate the mystery of the Incarnation from a perspective purposefully de-emphasizing the distant grandeur of God, in order to call attention to the *presence* of the Holy One. Images evoking the distant, "heavenly" or over-lord qualities of divinity (for example, phrases such as "new born King") are modified, since that manner of expressing honor conveys a style of power at odds with the self-humbling nature of incarnation.

It may at first surprise some singers that Mary is here recognized as revealer of God in her own person, rather than as simply an "instrument of the Lord." She is named as both mother of Jesus and true embodiment *herself* of the image of God! The more shocked we are at this notion, the more valuable it is as a way of calling forth appropriate astonishment at the very idea of Divine Incarnation. This viewpoint also stimulates us to consider that the Incarnation may be a more comprehensive event than we have here-to-fore imagined: an event in which God appears in human flesh of both genders.

In keeping with this appreciation that God's nature and God's actions are not gender-linked, care has been taken to neutralize those traditional modes of expression which gratuitously emphasize Jesus' maleness. Unless his gender is the significant factor, it is theologically more consistent to use language that does not call attention to the fact that he happens to be male.

As much as possible, archaic language forms have been replaced by standard contemporary usage; racially-oriented terms have been changed; the traditional "higher is better" imagery has been modified to reflect Jesus' own approval of "the least" as of great value. New wording emphasizes the expansive, welcoming, inclusive dimension of grace, which seeks to bless all alike—and honors the Earth as valid arena for spirituality.

Think of these modified carols not as corrections, but as complements to the traditional songs of the season you love so well. May they deepen and enhance your musical celebration of the Christmas miracle.

This book was developed as a resource for participational programs at Haelix Center in Scotland, Connecticut. Our powerful, inspiring pre-Christmas evening program can be recreated in your home or church by simply singing all these songs in sequence. They are arranged to weave a tapestry of the entire Christmas drama, from Advent anticipations of the event... to the announcement of "Joy to the World!"... through songs that tell the story of the shepherds, the angelic host, the Star, and the "wise men" or sages... then to Bethlehem and the Baby in the manger... and finally, songs that celebrate our response to the holy birth. We suggest that as a prelude to your program, the group practice the Round, "Child of the Living God"—so that it is already familiar when sung as the next-to-last selection of the evening. This song may also be done in call-and-response style. If your group wishes to share Communion together, Song 22 correlates well. A complete program outline is given at the end of this book.

The words of all the songs are set in large type, an important convenience allowing soft lighting or even candlelight for the program. The few selections with unfamiliar tunes have been transcribed onto musical staffs, using easy-to-read bold notes showing just the melody line, to be grasped most easily even by those without musical training. Chord notations suggest harmonies.

Feminist Sacred Songs for Christmas

Advent Songs

*The Divine Womb
prepares for the birth of the Christ-Child.
Wait and make ready!*

O Come, O Come Emmanuel

O come, O come Em-man-u-el
And ran-som cap-tive Is-ra-el,
That mourns in lone-ly ex-ile here,
Un-til the Child of God ap-pear.

> *Refrain:*
> Re-joice! Rejoice! Em-man-u-el
> Shall come to thee, O Is-ra-el!

O come, thou Day-spring, come and cheer
Our spir-its by thine Ad-vent here;
Dis-perse the gloom-y clouds of night,
And death's dark shad-ows put to flight.
Refrain

O come, thou Wis-dom from on high,
And or-der all things, far and nigh;
To us the path of know-ledge show,
And cause us in right ways to go.
Refrain

O come, De-sire of na-tions, bind
All peo-ples in one heart and mind;
Bid en-vy, strife, and quar-rels cease;
Fill the whole world with ho-ly peace.
Refrain

Feminist Sacred Songs for Christmas ©1994 by Genia Pauli Haddon. Reprinted only with permission. Plus Publications: 203-456-0646.

2 Wake, Awake!

Philipp Nicolai, 1556-1608
Alt. by Genia Pauli Haddon, 1989

WACHET AUF 8.9.8.8.8.9.8.6.6.4.8.8
Melody by Philipp Nicolai

A 1 Wake, a-wake, for night is fly-ing; The watch-ers on— the
B 2 Zi-on hears the watch-ers sing-ing; Her heart with deep de-
A-B 3 Now let ev-'ry tongue a-dore thee! Both men and wo—men

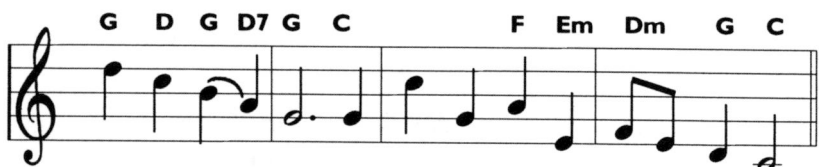

heights are cry——ing, A-wake, Je-ru-sa-lem,—— a-rise!
light is spring——ing. She wakes, she ris-es from— her gloom.
sing be-fore— Thee! Let harps and cym-bals now—— u-nite.

Mid-night's sol-emn hour is toll-ing; the char-iot wheels are
Christ, for whom she was cre-at-ed, her true be-lov———ed
All thy gates with pearl are glo-rious, fore-tell-ing heav-en-ly

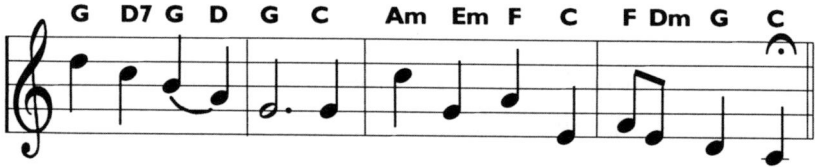

near-er roll——ing; Christ comes! O Church, lift up— thine eyes!
long-a-wait——ed, Her star is ris'n, her light— is come!
joys in store for us With-in the burn-ing Source of Light.

Feminist Sacred Songs for Christmas ©1994 by Genia Pauli Haddon. Reprinted only with permission. Plus Publications: 203-456-0646.

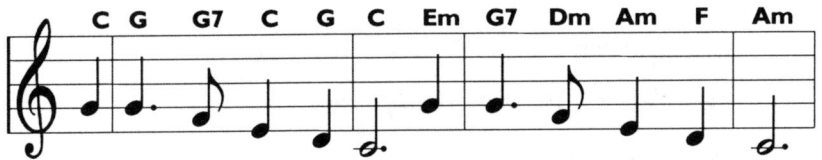

Rise up, with will-ing feet Go forth, the Bride-groom meet:
Ah, come thou bless-ed One, God's own be—lov—ed Son,
No vis-ion can fore-see That fi—nal ec-sta—sy.

Hal-le-lu-jah! Lo, great and small, We—an-swer all;
Hal-le-lu-jah! We haste a—long, An—ea-ger throng,
Hal-le-lu-jah! There-fore with joy our—song shall soar

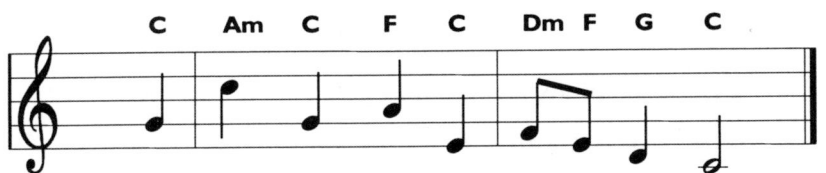

We fol-low where thy voice—shall call.
And glad-some join the ad—vent song.
In praise to God for-ev—er-more.

> *I am my beloved's, and his desire is for me.*
> *Come my beloved, let us go forth into the fields...*
> *There I will give you my love.*
> *Song of Solomon 7:10-12*

Feminist Sacred Songs for Christmas ©1994 by Genia Pauli Haddon. Reprinted only with permission. Plus Publications: 203-456-0646.

3   *Lift Up Your Heads*

Tune: TRURO L.M. *

Lift up your heads, ye might-y gates;
Be-hold, the Host in glo-ry waits!

The distant God is draw-ing near;
The Sav-ior of the world is here.

Fling wide the por-tals of your heart;
In-vite the bless-ing Christ [a-lone] im-parts.

With-in your soul a place pre-pare,
A-dorned with love and joy and prayer.

Re-deem-er come! I o-pen wide
My heart to thee; with-in a-bide!

Let me thine inner pres-ence feel;
Thy love and grace in me re-veal.

So come, my Sav-ior en-ter in!
Let new and no-bler life be-gin;

Thy Ho-ly Spir-it breathe in me;
'Til heart, mind, soul, [and strength,] I live as thee!

* Alternatives: "He Leadeth Me" without refrain.
Omitting parenthesized words, "Ride On, Ride On In Majesty!"

Feminist Sacred Songs for Christmas ©1994 by Genia Pauli Haddon. Reprinted only with permission. Plus Publications: 203-456-0646.

Come, Thou Long-Expected Jesus

Come, thou long-ex-pect-ed Je-sus
    Born to set all peo-ple free;
From our fears and sins re-lease us;
    Let us find our rest in thee.

Source of strength and con-so-la-tion,
    Hope of all the earth thou art;
Dear de-sire of ev-ery na-tion,
    Joy of ev-ery long-ing heart.

Born all captives to de-liv-er;
    Born a child, on earth to live;
Born to live in us for-ev-er;
    Now thy gra-cious free-dom give.

By thine own e-ter-nal Spir-it
    Mold our hearts to thee a-lone.
By thine all-suf-fi-cient mer-it
    Claim us now to be thine own.

5 Lullaby for the Expected Child

Irene Levine, 1989
Tune by Irene Levine

1 Lul-la-by, Lul-la-by. Babe of hope that grows in-side.
2 Lul-la-by, Lul-la-by. Babe of change that grows in-side.
3 Lul-la-by, Lul-la-by. Babe of joy that grows in-side.

How I wait for you to grow. Sea — sons pass be-fore I know
Who can guess how it will be When— you're here for all to see?
Wait-ing is so hard for me, My grow-ing, lit-le mys-ter-y.

When I'll see your smil-ing face, Fill-ing me with joy and grace.
I have man-y dreams for you. You'll have dreams to tell me, too.
I'll be glad when you are here, My won-drous, longed-for Ba-by dear.

Feminist Sacred Songs for Christmas ©1994 by Genia Pauli Haddon. Reprinted only with permission. Plus Publications: 203-456-0646.

Christmas Songs

*The Divine Womb
brings forth the Christ-Child.
Rejoice!*

Joy to the World!

Joy to the world! The Christ is here!
　　The gift of peace to bring!
Let ev-'ry heart a wel-come place pre-pare.
　　And heav'n and na-ture sing,
　　And heav'n and na-ture sing,
And hea-ven, and hea-ven and na-ture sing!

Joy to the Earth! The Sav-ior lives!
　　With song your voice employ;
While fields and floods, rocks, plains and hills
　　Re-peat the sound-ing joy,
　　Re-peat the sound-ing joy,
Re-peat, re-peat the sound-ing joy!

Christ fills the world with truth and grace,
　　And asks each life to prove
The glo-ries of God's right-eous-ness
　　And won-ders of God's love,
　　And won-ders of God's love,
And won-ders, and won-ders of God's love!

Feminist Sacred Songs for Christmas ©1994 by Genia Pauli Haddon. Reprinted only with permission. Plus Publications: 203-456-0646.

7 While Shepherds Watched Their Flocks

While shep-herds watched their flocks by night, B
All seat-ed on the ground,
A Mes-sen-ger of Light ap-peared,
And glo-ry shone a-round...

    "Fear not," a voice com-mand-ed them, A
    to soothe their awe-struck minds.
    "Glad tid-ings of great joy I bring
    to bless all hu-man-kind...

"To you, in Beth-le-hem is born A-B
In the ripe full-ness of time
The Sav-ior, who is Christ, the Word;
And this shall be the sign...

    "In a manger, wrapped in swath-ing cloths B
    The new-born babe is laid.
    Go, now, make haste to find the one
    For whom you long have prayed..."

Then with the Mes-sen-ger ap-peared A
A bril-liant, won-drous throng
Of ang-els prais-ing God, who thus
Ad-dressed their joy-ful song...

    "All glo-ry be to God on high, A-B
    And to the Earth be peace;
    Good will hence-forth from God to all
    Be-gin and nev-er cease...."

Feminist Sacred Songs for Christmas ©1994 by Genia Pauli Haddon. Reprinted only with permission. Plus Publications: 203-456-0646.

It Came Upon a Midnight Clear

It came up-on the mid-night clear,
> That glor-i-ous song of old.

From an-gels bending near the earth
> To touch their harps of gold;

"Peace on the Earth, good will to all,
> The gra-cious Christ-child brings."

The world in sol-emn still-ness lay
> To hear the an-gels sing.

Still through the clo-ven skies they come,
> With peace-ful wings un-furled,

And still their heav-en-ly mu-sic floats
> O'er all the wait-ing world;

A-bove its moun-tains and yearn-ing plains
> They bend on hov-er-ing wing,

And ev-er o'er its Ba-bel sounds
> The bles-sed an-gels sing.

For lo, the days are hasten-ing on,
> For cent-ur-ies now fore-told,

When with the ev-er cir-cling years
> Comes 'round the Age of Gold;

When peace shall o-ver all the Earth
> Its an-cient splen-dors fling,

And the whole world send back the song
> Which now the an-gels sing.

Feminist Sacred Songs for Christmas ©1994 by Genia Pauli Haddon. Reprinted only with permission. Plus Publications: 203-456-0646.

9 Angels From the Realms of Glory

An-gels, from the realms of glo-ry,   A-B
   Wing your flight o-er all the Earth;
Once you sang cre-a-tion's sto-ry,
   Now pro-claim Mes-si-ah's birth:

   Refrain: A-B
      Come and wor-ship, come and wor-ship,
      Word made flesh of Ma-ry's flesh.

Shep-herds, in the fields a-bid-ing,   A
   Watch-ing o'er your flocks by night,
Witness God—with—us re-sid-ing;
   Soft-ly shines the Infant Light: *Refrain*

Sa-ges, leave your con-tem-pla-tions,   B
   Bright-er vis-ions beam a-far;
Seek the great De-sire of na-tions,
   You have seen the na-tal star: *Refrain*

Saints, be-fore the al-tar kneel-ing,   A-B
   Watch-ing long in hope and trust;
Sud-den-ly the Word re-vealing
   God-eternal, here for us.   *Refrain*

Feminist Sacred Songs for Christmas ©1994 by Genia Pauli Haddon. Reprinted only with permission. Plus Publications: 203-456-0646.

Hark! The Herald Angels Sing

Hark! the her-ald an-gels sing, "Tid-ings of great joy we bring!
Peace on earth, and mer-cy mild, God and sin-ners rec-on-ciled!"
Join-ing in the an-gels' song, Raise your voic-es sure and strong;
With an-gel-ic hosts pro-claim, "Christ is born in Beth-le-hem!"

> *Refrain:*
> Hark! the her-ald an-gels sing,
> "Tid-ings of great joy we bring!"

U-ni-ver-sal-ly a-dored, Christ the ever-living Word,
Form-ing now in blood and bone, Off-spring of the Ho-ly Womb.
Veiled in flesh the God-head see; Hail the in-car-nate De-i-ty,
Pleased on Earth with us to dwell, Je-sus, our Em-man-u-el.

Refrain

Hail the low-ly Prince of Peace! Hail the Sun of Righteousness!
Light and life for all he wills, heal-ing ev-ery hu-man ill.
Mild, he lays his glo-ry by, Born that we no more may die;
Born to nur-ture us on Earth; Born to give us sec-ond birth.

Refrain

Feminist Sacred Songs for Christmas ©1994 by Genia Pauli Haddon. Reprinted only with permission. Plus Publications: 203-456-0646.

11 Angels We Have Heard on High

An-gels we have heard on high   B
Sweet-ly sing-ing o'er the plain.
And the moun-tains in re-ply   A
Ech-o back their joy-ous strains.

Refrain: A-B
   Glo————ri-a   In ex-cel-sis De-o.
   Glo————ri-a   In ex-cel-sis De-o.

Shep-herds, why this ju-bi-lee?   B
Why your joy-ous shouts pro-long?
Say, what may the ti-dings be,   A
Which in-spire your hap-py song?
                             Refrain

Come to Beth-le-hem and see   A-B
Here sal-va-tion has be-gun.
Come a-dore on bend-ed knee,
Christ, in flesh the Holy One.   *Refrain*

Feminist Sacred Songs for Christmas ©1994 by Genia Pauli Haddon. Reprinted only with permission. Plus Publications: 203-456-0646.

Creator of the Stars of Night   12

Tune: "Just As I Am"

Cre-a-tor of the stars of night,
Self-luminous, un-creat-ed Light!
We feel you stir in our in-ward parts.
We yearn to cra-dle you in our hearts.

To you the deep trav-ail was known
That made the whole cre-a-tion groan.
That labor long at last brings forth
The promised One, to bless the Earth.

The wait-ing world drew on t'ward night;
You came to it, not in splen-dor bright
As mon-arch, but as an infant born in
A humble place, on a winter's morn.

Feminist Sacred Songs for Christmas ©1994 by Genia Pauli Haddon. Reprinted only with permission. Plus Publications: 203-456-0646.

Lo, How a Rose Ever-Blooming

Lo, how a Rose e'er bloom-ing
　　From ten-der stem hath sprung!
Of Jes-se's lin-eage com-ing
　　As pro-phets long have sung.

It came, a flower-et bright,
　　A-mid the cold of win-ter,
　When half spent was the night.

I-sa-iah 'twas fore-told it,
　　The time appointed now has come.
With Mar-y we be-hold it,
　　Born of her ho-ly, hu-man womb.

To show God's love a-right,
　　　She bore the in-fant Sav-ior,
　When half spent was the night.

Feminist Sacred Songs for Christmas ©1994 by Genia Pauli Haddon. Reprinted only with permission. Plus Publications: 203-456-0646.

In Mary's Heart

Genia Pauli Haddon, 1994
Roberta Bitgood

Feminist Sacred Songs for Christmas ©1994 by Genia Pauli Haddon. Reprinted only with permission. Plus Publications: 203-456-0646.

What Star Is This?

Tune choices: PUER NOBIS NASCITOR or
"O Master, Let Me Walk with Thee" MARYTON,
or The Doxology, OLD HUNDREDTH

What star is this, with beams so bright,   A-B
More love-ly than the noon-day light?
It brings glad tid-ings of the birth,
Of God in hu-man form on Earth.

'Tis now ful-filled what God de-creed,   B
"From Ja-cob shall a star pro-ceed."
And lo! the east-ern sa-ges stand
To read in heav-en God's com-mand.

O Je-sus, while the star of grace   A
Im-pels us on to seek thy face,
Let not our sloth-ful hearts re-fuse
The guid-ance of thy Light to use.

To God e-ter-nal, heaven-ly Light,   A-B
To Christ, re-veal-ed in Earth-ly night,
To Spir-it, Holy Ghost we raise
An end-less song of thank-ful praise!

Feminist Sacred Songs for Christmas ©1994 by Genia Pauli Haddon. Reprinted only with permission. Plus Publications: 203-456-0646.

In the Bleak Mid-Winter

In the bleak mid-win-ter, Frost-y wind made moan,
Earth stood hard as i-ron, Wa-ter like a stone;
Snow had fall-en, snow on snow, Snow on snow,
In the bleak mid-win-ter, Long a-go.

Our God, heav'n can-not hold, Nor Earth sus-tain;
Heav'n and Earth shall flee a-way When love comes to reign.
In the bleak mid-win-ter A sta-ble place suf-ficed
To cra-dle God in-car-nate, Je-sus Christ.

An-gels and arch-an-gels May have gath-ered there,
Cher-u-bim and ser-a-phim Thronged the air;
But the wom-an Ma-ry In ma-ter-nal bliss,
Wor-shipped the be-lov-ed With a kiss.

What can I give Christ, Poor as I am?
If I were a shep-herd I would bring a lamb;
If I were a "Wise Man*," I would do my part;
Yet what I have I give Christ— Give my heart.

* or substitute *sage*

Feminist Sacred Songs for Christmas ©1994 by Genia Pauli Haddon. Reprinted only with permission. Plus Publications: 203-456-0646.

O Little Town of Bethlehem

O lit-tle town of Beth-le-hem, A-B
How still we see thee lie!
A-bove thy deep and dream-less sleep
The si-lent stars go by;
Yet in thy dark streets shin-eth
The ev-er-last-ing Light;
The hopes and fears of all the years
Are met in thee to-night.

For Christ is born of Ma-ry, B
And gath-er-ed all a-bove,
While mor-tals sleep, the an-gels keep
Their watch of won-d'ring love.
O morn-ing stars, to-geth-er A
Pro-claim the ho-ly birth!
Your rays so bright announce the Light
of Peace to all on Earth.

A-B

How si-lent-ly, how si-lent-ly,
The won-drous gift is giv'n!
So God im-parts to hu-man hearts
The bless-ed peace of heav'n.
No ear may hear Christ's com-ing
But in this world of sin,
When meek souls will re-ceive God, still
The dear Christ en-ters in.

A-B

O ho-ly Child of Beth-le-hem!
En-liv-en us, we pray;
Cast out our sin and en-ter in;
Be born in us to-day.
We hear the Christ-mas an-gels
The great glad tid-ings tell;
O come to us, a-bide with us,
Our God Em-man-u-el!

Feminist Sacred Songs for Christmas ©1994 by Genia Pauli Haddon. Reprinted only with permission. Plus Publications: 203-456-0646.

Bring a Torch, Jeannette, Isabella!

Bring a torch, Jean-ette, Is-a-bel-la!
Bring a torch, to the cra-dle—and run!
  It is Je-sus, good folk of the vil-lage;
  Christ is born and Ma-ry's call-ing.
    Ah! Ah! Beau-ti-ful is the mo-ther!
    Ah! Ah! Beau-ti-ful is her son!

It is wrong when the child is sleep-ing,
It is wrong to talk so loud;
  Si-lence, all, as you gath-er a-round,
  Lest your noise should wa-ken Je-sus.
    Hush! Hush! See how the child is sleep-ing.
    Hush! Hush! See how fast he sleeps!

Soft-ly now to the lit-tle sta-ble,
Soft-ly here for a mo-ment come;
  Look and see how charm-ing is Je-sus,
  Fat and round and sweet and tender.
    Hush! Hush! See how the child is sleep-ing;
    Hush! Hush! See how he smiles in dreams.

Feminist Sacred Songs for Christmas ©1994 by Genia Pauli Haddon. Reprinted only with permission. Plus Publications: 203-456-0646.

What Child is This?

A
What child is this, who laid to rest
   On Ma-ry's lap is sleep-ing?
Whom an-gels greet with an-thems sweet,
   While shep-herds watch are keep-ing?

A-B
Refrain
   This, this is the Word made flesh
      Whom shep-herds guard and an-gels bless.
   Haste, haste to bring them love,
      The Babe and the Moth-er, Ma-ry.

B
Why rest they here in such pov-er-ty
   Where ox and ass are feed-ing?
Good Christian, fear: for sin-ners here
   The si-lent Word is plead-ing.   *Refrain*

Feminist Sacred Songs for Christmas ©1994 by Genia Pauli Haddon. Reprinted only with permission. Plus Publications: 203-456-0646.

Away in a Manger

A-way in a man-ger, no crib for a bed,
The Lit-tle One, Je-sus, laid down his sweet head.
The stars in the sky looked down where he lay,
The Little One, Je-sus, a-sleep on the hay.

The cat-tle are low-ing, the Ba-by a-wakes.
But dear lit-tle Je-sus, no cry-ing he makes.
"I love you, sweet Je-sus. Be with me, I pray;
And stay by my cra-dle un-til break of day."

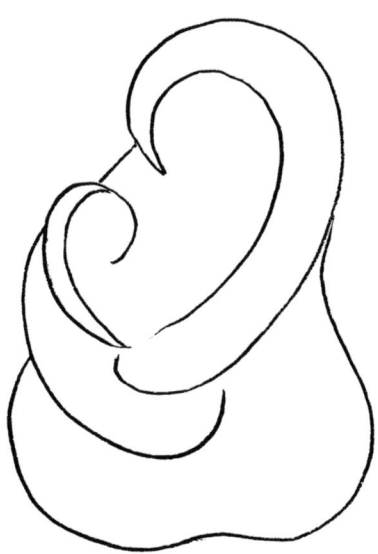

Feminist Sacred Songs for Christmas ©1994 by Genia Pauli Haddon. Reprinted only with permission. Plus Publications: 203-456-0646.

Silent Night

Si-lent night, ho-ly night,
All is calm, all is bright
> 'Round yon vir-gin moth-er and child.
> Ho-ly in-fant so ten-der and mild,

Sleep in heav-en-ly peace,
Sleep in heav-en-ly peace.

Si-lent night, ho-ly night,
Shep-herds quake at the sight,
> Glo-ries stream from heav-en a-far,
> Heav'n-ly hosts sing al-le-lu-ia;

Christ, the Savior, is born!
Christ, the Savior, is born!

Si-lent night, ho-ly night,
Child of God, love's pure light
> Ra-diance beams from thy ho-ly face,
> With the dawn of re-deem-ing grace,

Je-sus Christ at thy birth,
Je-sus Christ at thy birth.

Feminist Sacred Songs for Christmas ©1994 by Genia Pauli Haddon. Reprinted only with permission. Plus Publications: 203-456-0646.

22 Let All Mortal Flesh Keep Silence

Liturgy of St. James, 19th century, vs. 1 & 2, alt.
Genia Pauli Haddon, vs. 3 & 4, 1988

PICARDY 8.7.8.7.8.7.
Traditional French melody, 17th century

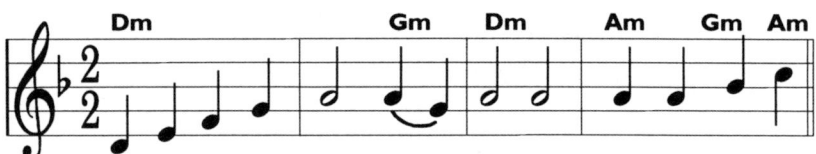

1 Let all mor-tal flesh ke-ep si-lence, And with fear and
2 Ful-ly God, yet born of— Ma-ry. As of old on
3 Bread is bro-ken, Christ is— with us, "This, my bo-dy:
4 Christ in-car-nate, Christ e———ter-nal, Christ the ho-ly,

trem-bling— stand; Pon-der noth-ing earth-ly— mind-ed,
earth he——— stood, Word di-vine in hu-man— ves-ture,
Take and— eat." In the cup poured out we dis-cern him
Christ the— whole. Christ the heal-er, Christ res-ur-rect-ed,

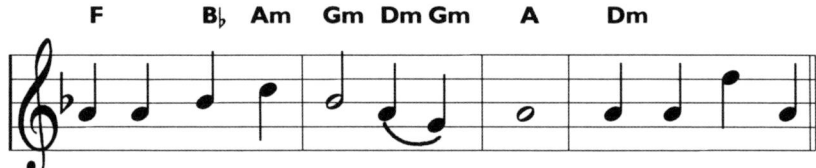

For with bless-ings In both— hands, Christ our God to
In the bo-dy and the— blood, He will give to
Ho-ly, emp-tied, pres-ent, com-plete. Turn and see the
Christ ful-fill-ing all fore———told. Al-le-lu-ia,

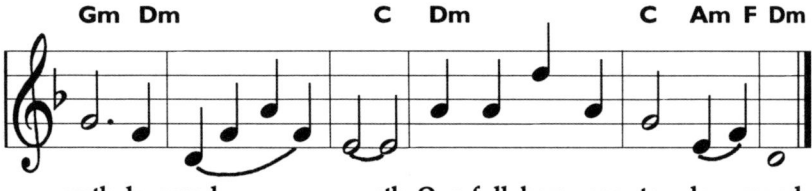

earth de-scend————eth, Our full hom-age to de— mand.
all the faith————ful His own self for heav-en-ly food.
Christ be-fore, be-side, be-hind you; Christ in ev'-ry-one you— meet.
Al-le-lu————ia, Christ my ver-y Self, my— soul.

Feminist Sacred Songs for Christmas ©1994 by Genia Pauli Haddon. Reprinted only with permission. Plus Publications: 203-456-0646.

O Come, All Ye Faithful   23

A-B   O come, all ye faith-ful, joy-ful and tri-um-phant,
      O come ye, O come ye to Beth-le-hem;
      Come and be-hold this child born of Ma-ry.

> *Refrain:*
> B   O come, let us a-dore them;
> A   O come, let us a-dore them;
> A-B O come, let us a-dore them:
>   Mo-ther and Child.

A-B   Sing, choirs of an-gels, sing in ex-ul-ta-tion,
      Sing, all you mes-sen-ger's of God's ho-ly word.
      Glo-ry to God In-car-nate, all glo-ry.
                                          Refrain

A-B   Christ-child, we greet thee, born this happy morning,
      Born of the Wo-man Ma-ry, Mo-ther of God!
      Word of Cre-a-tion, now in flesh ap-pear-ing;
                                          Refrain

Feminist Sacred Songs for Christmas ©1994 by Genia Pauli Haddon. Reprinted only with permission. Plus Publications: 203-456-0646.

24   *Good Christian Friends, Rejoice*

Good Chris-tian friends, re-joice,
    With heart and soul and voice;
Give good heed to what we say:
    Je-sus Christ is born to-day;
Ox and ass be-fore him bow,
    And he is in the man-ger now.
Christ is born to-day! Christ is born to-day!

Good Chris-tian friends, re-joice,
    With heart and soul and voice;
You are of-fered end-less bliss;
    Je-sus Christ was born for this!
God has opened wide the door,
    And you are blessed for-ev-er-more.
Christ was born for this! Christ was born for this!

Good Chris-tian friends, re-joice,
    With heart and soul and voice;
Now you need not fear the grave;
    Je-sus Christ was born to save!
Draws you safe, se-cure, and warm
    Into the ev-er-last-ing arms.
Christ was born to save! Christ was born to save!

Feminist Sacred Songs for Christmas ©1994 by Genia Pauli Haddon. Reprinted only with permission. Plus Publications: 203-456-0646.

Christians, Awaken! 25

Tune choices: YORKSHIRE or
"Be Still My Soul" FINLANDIA

A-B　Christians, awaken, greet anew the morn
　　Whereon the Savior of the world was born;
　　　　Rise to adore the mystery of love,
　　　　Which hosts of angels chanted from above;
　　With them the joyful news was first begun
　　Of God incarnate, Mother Mary's Son.

A　　　　Then to the watchful shepherds it was told,
　　　　Who heard th' angelic herald's voices bold:
　　　　　　"I bring good tidings of a Savior's birth
　　　　　　To you and all the nations upon earth;
　　　　Strong Mary has revealed God's faithfulness;
　　　　This day is born the Christ, in human flesh."

B　　The shepherds ran to Bethlehem to find
　　God–with–us, in disguise as humankind.
　　　　And found, with Joseph and the blessed maid,
　　　　Her Son, the Savior, in a manger laid;
　　Amazed, the wondrous story they proclaimed,
　　The first apostles of his infant fame.

A-B　　　　O may we keep and ponder in our mind
　　　　God's wondrous love in saving humankind:
　　　　　　Trace we the babe, Who has retrieved our loss,
　　　　　　From that poor manger to the bitter cross;
　　　　Treading the way assisted by God's grace,
　　　　Till our first heavenly state again takes place.

Feminist Sacred Songs for Christmas ©1994 by Genia Pauli Haddon. Reprinted only with permission. Plus Publications: 203-456-0646.

All Who Tell the Gospel Story

Tune: "Angels From the Realms of Glory"

All who tell the gos-pel sto-ry,
    All who join the pil-grim search,
All who sing cre-a-tion's glory,
    Wel-come now the Savior's birth.

Refrain:
Come and wor-ship, come and wor-ship,
Let new prais-es fill the Earth!

Sa-ges, leave your con-tem-pla-tion;
    Let the still, small voice be heard,
Speak-ing peace a-mong the na-tions;
    Can you hear the won-drous word? *Refrain*

Lo, there comes a shep-herd gath'ring
    Least and lost unto the fold.
Can you hear the trum-pet call-ing,
    As it did in days of old? *Refrain*

To the wea-ry comes re-fresh-ment;
    To the griev-ing, strength and peace;
To the anx-ious, sweet con-tent-ment;
    To the cap-tive soul, re-lease. *Refrain*

Feminist Sacred Songs for Christmas ©1994 by Genia Pauli Haddon. Reprinted only with permission. Plus Publications: 203-456-0646.

Child of the Living God

27

Lorraine M. Nelson, 1992

Lorraine M. Nelson
Original key: A

I am a child— of the liv-ing— God; I breathe beau-ty all a-long my way.

I am the light of the di - vine— flame, Grow-ing bright-er ev -'ry day.

I am the love— that— fills my soul-, Shar-ing joy and peace— with— all.

To use as a Chant, sing each line twice—first as "call," then as "response."
May also be sung as a 3-part or 6-part Round.

28 Joy, Peace, and Love! The Gifts of Christ!

Tune: "Joy to the World!"

Joy, Peace, and Love! The gifts of Christ!
    Peace, Free-dom, Love, and Joy!
Faith, pa-tience, hope, hu-mil-i-ty.
Grace, wis-dom, truth, tran-quil-li-ty.
    Re-ceive the gifts of God.
    Re-ceive the gifts of God.
Christ comes, Christ gives the gifts of God.

Just-ice for all, and ec-sta-sy,
Con-tent-ment, growth, and bliss.
Life, good-ness, power, and gen-tle-ness.
Strength, kind-ness, health, and con-scious-ness.
    These gifts be born in you.
    These gifts be born in you.
Re-ceive, re-ceive—and give a-new!

Evening Program Outline

INVITATIONS: Choose a date near Christmas or Epiphany, allowing two hours total. Let those you invite know in advance that *non-traditional* versions of Christmas songs will be sung. A good introduction would be to send each person a copy of the "Theological and Practical Guidelines" from the front of this book. *Call Plus Publications, (203)456-0646, for permission.* Suggestion: Ask each one to bring a wrapped heart-gift—such as a sampler of home-baked seasonal goodies, a tree ornament, or a copy of a favorite poem—for giving away during the program, as a symbol of the Divine giving.

SETTING UP: •If possible arrange seating in a circle, to emulate the surroundment of the Divine Womb. •Lighting should be soft; just bright enough to read songbooks. •Simple centerpiece of greens, candles, etc., with space for placing the basket of "Gift Certificates."

EQUIPMENT AND MATERIALS NEEDED:
•Stereo tape player, with cassette of song-accompaniments, recorded in sequence; *or* a musician to provide piano/guitar accompaniment.
•For Communion, provide *broken* bread (rather than cut—to match words of the song!) and wine (or grape juice); on small trays for easy passing.
•A stack of 3"x5" cards, pencils for writing out "Gift Certificates"—and a basket or tray for collecting them.
•Songbooks for everybody.

As guests arrive, have tape of Song 27 playing in background, to begin making the tune familiar. (To order Lorraine Nelson's album *Into the Hands of God* call Kripalu-by-Mail, 800-967-7279.) Arriving guests place their wrapped gifts around centerpiece.

Preliminaries: •Briefly describe the purpose of the evening, basing your comments on the material on pages 9-11 in this book.
•Practice Song 27 - Learning *well* just the individual lines, separately.
•Divide participants into "A" and "B" groups. [Note: if there are approximately equal numbers of men and women, have the men form Group "A", the women Group "B". Otherwise, just divide the circle in half.] Explain that many of the songs have marginal cues, showing which group is to sing that verse or line.

PROGRAM SCRIPT (Using *An Inclusive-Language Lectionary*, by Nat'l Council of the Churches of Christ)

Song 1

SCRIPTURE: James 5:7-8

Personal sharings - What have times of waiting been like in our own lives—especially the nine months of pregnancy?

"The Divine Womb prepares for the birth of the Christ-Child.
    Wait and make ready!"   (All heavy italics to be spoken by a leader.)

Songs 2-5

SCRIPTURES: Luke 1:39-42 *and* Luke 2:1-14
"The Divine Womb brings forth the Christ-Child. Rejoice!"
Songs 6-11

Gather in small groups, to plan and fill out "Gift Certificates."
"What will you offer to God?" With the support of your group, identify your own growing edge. Choose some specific aspect of your life, relating to that edge, which you are willing to offer consciously to the Divine: a risk, a talent, a commitment, etc. Write it on the 3"x5" card, as your Gift Certificate for the Christ-child.

Return to full circle.
SCRIPTURES: Matthew 2:1-2, 9b-11 *and* Luke 2:14-20
Songs 12-16
Naming our Gifts-of-Heart to Christ - Pass basket. Each one puts in card, either naming the gift out loud or saying, "What I have, I give." Place filled basket at center.
Songs 17-21

Consecrate and distribute **Elements for Communion**; *wait to eat/drink.*
Song 22, verses 1 & 2
Partaking of the Bread and Cup: *"The Word became flesh and blood, and dwelt among us. Remembering, marvelling, we eat this bread and drink this cup, as that divine body and blood."*
Song 22, verses 3 & 4
"Incarnation continues! Look around you at the many faces of God."

Songs 23-27 (Do Song 27 first as call-&-response and then as a Round.)
All stand, and each one chooses a wrapped gift from center, signifying the intention to receive responsibly the gifts of Christ. (Remain standing to the end.)
Song 28
Closing circle. Standing, hands linked
Benediction: *"Joy, peace, and love be born in you. Receive; receive—and give anew. A-men."*   Guests may continue *exchanging* their gifts, with each farewell.

Acknowledgments

ROBERTA BITGOOD - Award-winning composer, organ recitalist, and church musician for more than six decades, Dr. Bitgood has often been a pioneer in her field. She was the first woman to earn a doctorate from the Union Theological Seminary School of Sacred Music, and the only woman ever chosen as president of the American Guild of Organists. Her anthem, "Give me a Faith" and a wedding song, "The Greatest of These is Love" are classic favorites. She composed the music for "In Mary's Heart" especially for this new edition. Roberta has graciously transcribed the other original compositions in this volume, as well.

IRENE LEVINE - Folk guitarist, vocalist, and founding member of WomanChurch-East, Irene has composed many songs reflecting her own spiritual journey. "Lullaby for the Expected Child", included here as an Advent song, was originally written as gift for a WomanChurch sister during a time of profound personal change.

LORRAINE M. NELSON - Widely known as Bhavani, this talented vocalist travels the world giving workshops on freeing the voice, sounding for healing, and singing to God. A long-time resident of Kripalu Center, she shares her gifts there in concerts and chanting, and through her week-long sound immersion program, The Sound Self. "Child of the Living God", which reflects both her deep Christian roots and the influence of Eastern chant, has been published in the book *One God, Many Names* (Plus Publications: 1994) and also in the stereo album, *Into the Hands of God*. Lorraine's several albums may be ordered from Kripalu-by-Mail, 1-800-967-7279.

STEPHEN C. ROSE - A graduate of Union Theological Seminary, Stephen has written hundreds of Christian songs with fresh, graceful lyrics. Many of these have been published in anthologies. He is a prolific author of books and articles on Christian faith, and edits a daily cyberspace newsletter targeting the interplay of theological and social issues.

About the Editor-Author

GENIA PAULI HADDON is an ordained minister of the United Church of Christ. She served as a Pastor in several churches, and then a fifteen-year ministry providing spiritual counseling to individuals and couples, before retiring from formal ministry in 1991 to teach and write. She holds the Doctor of Ministry degree in pastoral counseling and Ph.D. in Jungian psychology, having studied briefly at the C.G. Jung Institute in Zurich during 1978 and 1980. She is a member of the adjunct faculty for the doctoral program of the Union Institute.

Her personal spiritual development has been nurtured also through several non-traditional trainings. In the process of solidly integrating each, she gains the necessary certifications to be be able to teach others what has worked for herself.

She has studied under Yogi Amrit Desai and the senior staff at Kripalu Center, earning advanced-level certification as a Kripalu Yoga teacher in 1990. That year, she and another teacher created the videos *Yoga for Round Bodies 1 & 2*. She teaches spiritually-oriented yoga classes at Haelix, occasionally assisting with programs at Kripalu Center, as well.

A Hemi-Sync Trainer certified by The Monroe Institute, Faber, VA, Genia trained with out-of-body expert Robert A. Monroe, who is the creator of Hemi-Sync audio technology for the development of consciousness. Genia and her life-partner, Warren Haddon, together design and present Hemi-Sync supported programs for personal and spiritual development. Dr. Haddon was accepted into anthropologist Michael Harner's *Three-year Advanced Training in Shamanic Healing*, transferring after the first year into the training program at The Monroe Institute.

Genia was one of the founding members of WomanChurch-East. She is the author of numerous articles and books. Her work is counted among the most mature efforts of feminism to develop a new life philosopy.

The Feminist-Christian Resources Series

This collection honors the deepest, truest roots of Christian faith, while offering non-traditional expressions and interpretations. Those who are well-pleased with traditional views of Jesus Christ, of the Divine, and of the masculine Trinity, may find these unfamiliar forms offensive. Our intention is not to disturb those who are still powerfully moved by the old formulations, but to provide resources for those whose souls need new language and new forms for honoring the Divine in fullness.

Other Titles in the Feminist-Christian Resources Series

One God, Many Names: Inspirational Songs and Hymns
Genia Pauli Haddon, D.Min., Ph.D.

Haddon is a retired minister with 25 years of service in a Protestant denomination. Her Preface to this collection of inspirational songs provides a clear basis for moving beyond "inclusive language" that merely neuters pronouns, to new images of God drawn as much from womanly truth as from manly identity. Without sacrificing the original feeling or meaning, Haddon's revisions of old hymns achieve "perfection of non-sexist, all-inclusive, non-denominational language of... incredible power, charm, and grace."—*New Age Retailer*. Also includes new songs, never before in print, composed by several talented writers.

$10.95 + $1.50 shipping   ISBN 1-881311-24-4

Woman as Herself: Birthing Daughter/Goddess
Bernice Marie-Daly, Ph.D.

For each woman and for humankind, here is the blueprint for recovering our lost spiritual Self in the form of the adult Daughter. Guided by this sacred image, women will claim their full power, integrity and self-worth as persons. The ultimate result: expansion of human consciousness itself, with new ways of relating to Self, to faith traditions, to one another, to the natural world, to the cosmos. Dr. Marie-Daly is co-author of *Created In Her Image: Models of the Feminine Divine*, and founder of *Awakenings: The New School for Women's Spirituality*.

$16.95 + $1.75 shipping   ISBN 1-881311-30-9

Count-Down to Christmas
ADVENT CELEBRATIONS FOR FAMILIES WITH CHILDREN AGE 3-8
Warren D. Haddon, M.S. and Genia Pauli Haddon, D.Min., Ph.D.

Children are captivated by re-creating the Christmas story week by week, using Creche figures, candles, and other simple props to enact key meanings. Encourages reverent regard for the Earth by calling attention to the role of stars, animals, and the very stones in welcoming the Christ-child. Written in simple language, without gender bias. Detailed guidance for creating five family programs, one for each of the four weeks of Advent, plus at Christmas. The Haddons bring New Age insights to a lifetime of Christian faith, he as a dedicated layperson, she as an ordained minister for 25 years.

$10.95 + $1.50 shipping   ISBN 1-881311-12-0

TO ORDER: Send Check for products and shipping to:
Plus Publications, Box 265 Suite 94, Scotland CT 06264
CT purchasers, add State Sales Tax. Prices subject to change without notice.

Supportive Resources for Spiritually Aware Living

Uniting Sex, Self & Spirit   Genia Pauli Haddon, D.Min., Ph.D.

Understand changing sexual patterns and your personal role in the evolution of humankind. Heal relationships to others, the Earth, the Divine, and yourself. The author's credentials in Jungian psychology, counseling, biology, religion, shamanic healing, and yoga undergird ideas that are breathtakingly new, yet based on the wisdom we all carry in our own bodies. Foreword by Georg Feuerstein, who calls this work "Visionary..." Marion Woodman promises, "You will read this book with visceral response...Illuminating!" *New Age Retailer* praises this "incredible master work" as "destined best-seller...an undeniable classic."
$15.95 + $1.75 shipping   ISBN 1-881311-13-9

Writings by Re   Marie VanDuyne

This inspirational journal shares wisdom from The Guide, as received by a woman of great soul during the final years of her long life. The Guide says:

"This is my song in praise of all that is!...This is my offering to all who care..."

An exceptional gift for those on limitless spiritual journeys. Daily readings, with poems to punctuate the months.
$14.50 + $2.50 shipping   ISBN 1-881311-27-9

Yoga for Round Bodies 1 & 2   VIDEO COURSE
Linda DeMarco & Genia Pauli Haddon, Certified Kripalu Yoga Teachers

Enjoy the physical and subtle benefits of yoga right now, just as you are! Classic postures, adjusted to the needs of the ample figure by round-bodied teachers. Each volume contains three half-hour sessions, interweaving options for Beginner and Intermediate levels. Features music by Steve Roach. Nationally praised by *New Age Journal; BBW; Radiance; Yoga Journal; New Age Retailer.*
VHS, nearly 3 hours! 2-vol.Set - $59 + $2.25 shipping.   ISBN 1-881311-04-X

The Art of Living   INSPIRATIONAL CARD DECK   by Haelix

A powerful supplementary resource, whatever your spiritual path. Daily exploration of each inspiring affirmation takes you deeper into joyful, enlightened living. Elegantly packaged in richly patterned wallet with velcro closure. Six different designs, each subtly accented with gold. You'll love choosing just the right sets for all your friends! *Mauve Paisley, Ruby Harvest, Chrysanthemum, Vibrant Paisley, Native Rhythms, Butterfly.*
$10.95 + $1 shipping   ISBN 1-881311-21-X

At New Age bookstores nationwide and in Canada.
See prior page for how to order by mail from Plus Publications.